THIS BOOK BELONGS TO:

....

SPRING CLEANING

SPRING CLEANING

THE SPIRIT OF KEEPING HOME

by MONICA NASSIF :: photographs by PATRICK FOX

CHRONICLE BOOKS

SAN FRANCISCO

ACKNOWLEDGMENTS

First, I am grateful to the talented and dedicated people who completed this project swiftly and beautifully: Patrick Fox, photographer; Lisa Evidon, photo stylist; Heidi Madsen, photo stylist assistant; Robyn Warmbo and Darcy Shields Weinstine, book designers and art directors; Ellen Shaffer, whose finesse of language is exquisite; and Mikyla Bruder, our editor at Chronicle Books for her vision and editorial wisdom. Second, many thanks to my family and business partner. Frankly, I am a slob at heart who must work doubly hard to live a tidy life. Even though I relish large cleaning projects, I struggle with daily maintenance. My husband, thank you for being our vigilant neat freak, and my two daughters, thank you for completing your chore list before heading out to play. Also, thanks to Mary Dearing, my business partner, who believed in the Caldrea concept when it was a tiny gem of an idea and made it a reality. Amazing, lovely work—thank you.

Library of Congress Cataloging-in-Publication Data available.

ISBN: 0-8118-3985-0

Manufactured in China

Styled by **Lisa Evidon**

Designed by **Warmbo Design**

Distributed in Canada by Raincoast Books
9050 Shaughnessy Street
Vancouver, British Columbia V6P 6E5

10 9 8 7 6 5 4 3 2 1

Chronicle Books LLC
85 Second Street
San Francisco, California 94105
www.chroniclebooks.com

CONTENTS

 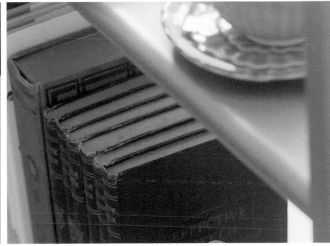

INTRODUCTION

The urge arrives several weeks before it's warm enough to open windows, on the first nice day when an extra glint of sunlight draws attention to a cobweb in a corner or a streak on the floor caused by tracked-in slush. The coziness of winter has given way to clutter.

Other things start to catch your eye: piles of outerwear in the hallway, fingerprints on the woodwork, or a stack of mail that has taken on a life of its own. The coat closet is stuffed beyond capacity, mostly with things that aren't coats. The space once occupied by the coffee table is now engulfed with piles of periodicals. All these signs point to one thing: It's time for spring cleaning. But you have no idea where to start or when to find the time.

Traditionally "spring cleaning" was done all at once. All the windows were thrown open and scrubbed clean. All the bedding was aired. All the rugs were hung on outdoor lines and beaten to drive the dirt away.

We still tend to think of spring cleaning as an all-or-nothing operation, a heap of tedious chores that does not stop until every speck of dirt is banished from our doorstep. It's enough to fill a weekend at least. No wonder spring cleaning has become a lost art—few of us can find the time for it!

But there's another way to approach spring cleaning. With the right mind-set, you can use your cleaning rituals as opportunities for mental spring cleaning as well. After all, caring for your home is really an extension of caring for yourself. And clearing away cobwebs is a terrific inspiration for clearing away outmoded ideas—like old-fashioned standards of domestic perfection, for instance.

Think of it as an occasion to celebrate: to shake the dust from the cushions, put the heavy woolens into storage, chase the cobwebs from the corners, clean out the closets, pack up outgrown clothes and toys, and throw open those windows to let in the fresh breezes of the first warm day.

Spring cleaning also helps you to set the stage for other springtime celebrations. Perhaps you'll be hosting a wedding shower, a birthday breakfast, or a special dinner. Even if you don't have any formal entertaining on your calendar, you can celebrate a freshly polished marble mantel with a cheery bouquet of tulips—or a freshly scrubbed kitchen with a basket full of lemons from the farmers' market.

Tradition notwithstanding, there's no rule that says spring cleaning has to be achieved in one relentless, joyless campaign. Try breaking it up into pieces: a room at a time, a task at a time, a half hour at a time. Then equip yourself with cleaners and tools that are as pleasant to use as they are effective. And enjoy each completed accomplishment as its own fresh start.

Of course, if your schedule permits, feel free to set aside a Saturday or a whole weekend. The key to spring cleaning is to adapt it to fit your life, rather than trying to adapt your life to fit an outmoded tradition.

So put on some music that makes you happy. Pick a place to start. And do as much—or as little—as you like!

1

GETTING ORGANIZED

How to create room-by-room plans, assemble the right tools for every task, and dress for success.

Good order is the foundation of all things.
— EDMUND BURKE

SPRING CLEANING IS A BIG UNDERTAKING. IF YOU JUST start tackling projects at random, you will soon run into snags. Perhaps you'll need to keep running to the store for tools and supplies. Maybe you'll scrub your kitchen floor before realizing that cleaning your oven will probably mess it up again. Or perhaps you'll just get overwhelmed.

But you can bring spring cleaning down to size with two simple tools: a notebook and a pen. Start by opening all the curtains and shades, to let in as much daylight as possible. Then walk around your home, notebook in hand, and write down what you see.

Be specific—and constructive! "Front hallway may be eligible for federal disaster relief funds" may be accurate, but it isn't helpful. Zero in on details, like removing cobwebs from the corners, changing burned-out lightbulbs, spot cleaning scuff marks on the wall, polishing brass or silver fixtures, and cleaning mirrors.

Spend at least five minutes in each room and really look at your surroundings—in the spaces we occupy every day, it's easy to just stop seeing things, especially things that need cleaning. Make a list for every room in your home. Then make yourself a cup of tea and sit down with your notebook. Go back to each task and note how much time you think it will take and what supplies you need.

After you finish your notes for each room, compile a master shopping list so that you can pick up everything you'll need in one convenient, efficient trip to the store. Then take a look at the time estimates for each room and make some scheduling decisions. If you know you'll have two hours on Saturday morning to clean the front hallway, write it on your calendar.

If a span of two uninterrupted hours seems like an unimaginable luxury, take the list one task at a time. Whenever you get five free minutes, you can simply check off any tasks that can be done in that time or, even better, prioritize according to how much the undone task is bothering you. If noticing the burned-out lightbulbs sets your teeth on edge every time you pass through the hallway, tackle that task first. If you need a high-powered flashlight to see the cobwebs in the corners, save them for later.

A SOUNDTRACK FOR SPRING CLEANING

Aerobics instructors, those paragons of perkiness, have long known that lively, interesting music can lift your mood and move your feet. If you're having trouble warming up to the very idea of spring cleaning, try using music to shift your attitude.

Use jazz and soul selections for reflective, meditative tasks such as cleaning out bookcases, closets, and drawers:

Belly of the Sun, Cassandra Wilson

Blue Gardenia, Etta James

Cesaria, Cesaria Evora

Dream, Jimmy Scott

Great Songs & Performances that Inspired the Motown 25th Anniversary, Marvin Gaye

Choose majestic, sweeping operatic music to create a conquering, powerful mood for cleaning the basement:

The Best of the Three Tenors, Carerras, Domingo, Pavarotti

If You Love Me, Cecilia Bartoli

Puccini's Heroines, Giacomo Puccini

Romanza, Andrea Bocelli

Tosca, featuring Maria Callas

For tasks that take a lot of energy, such as washing windows or cleaning out the refrigerator, borrow some sass and attitude from the masters of rock 'n' roll:

Anthology, Chuck Berry

Live 1975–1985, Bruce Springsteen

Riding with the King, Eric Clapton and B.B. King

Sticky Fingers, The Rolling Stones

Tina Live in Europe, Tina Turner

1. DRESS CODE

There's absolutely nothing wrong with the tried-and-true standard ensemble: old shirt plus old pants plus old sneakers. But the addition of a couple accessories will make spring cleaning easier and safer.

Dust mask   Even if you're not allergic to dust, why sneeze and wheeze if you don't have to?

Footwear   Sturdy, supportive, lace-up shoes are essential for maintaining comfort and forestalling fatigue.

Gloves   Protect your hands and nails from wear and tear. Use lightweight cotton for dry chores, sturdy latex for wet chores.

Headgear   A bandanna or baseball cap will keep cleaners and dust out of your hair.

Portable pockets   A carpenter's or gardener's apron will carry tools and supplies wherever you go.

Safety glasses or goggles   Protect your eyes from dust and sprays, especially if you wear contact lenses.

If you're taking a five-minutes-here-ten-minutes-there approach to spring cleaning, it will make very little sense to change clothes every time you have a spare moment to pick up a broom. Consider buying a chef's jacket at a restaurant supply store or gourmet shop. Then just keep it on a hook in your utility closet to grab whenever you want to protect what you're wearing from dust bunnies.

2. TOOLS

Good tools are well worth the investment, whether you're doing seasonal tasks or everyday cleaning. A tool that is lovely to behold results in a chore that is a pleasure to perform. Quality tools also deliver quality results and last far longer than their inexpensive counterparts.

BROOMS: Your cleaning cabinet should contain at least a couple of brooms. A traditional corn broom is an appealing choice for indoor chores like sweeping the kitchen floor because it's attractive and easy to clean. For more rugged outdoor jobs like porches, sidewalks, and driveways, invest in a push broom with water-resistant fibers.

BRUSHES, KITCHEN: Natural fiber cleaning brushes for the kitchen are a little more difficult to find than their synthetic counterparts. But they are worth seeking out. Keep a long, cylindrical bottle brush by your sink to clean bottles and vases. A shorter, thicker cylindrical brush is a handy tool for washing glasses quickly and effectively. You may also want to keep an inexpensive toothbrush or two in your kitchen for cleaning grime out of appliance crevices.

BRUSHES, SCRUB: Natural fiber bristles are the preferred choice, not only because they are more aesthetically appealing, but also because they hold water better. Synthetic bristles just push water around. Look for lightweight models with handles that fit comfortably in your hand.

BUCKETS: Plastic buckets may be cheaper and more lightweight, but a galvanized steel bucket will stand up to decades of abuse and still look nice enough to serve as an ice bucket for a casual cookout. Stock your home with at least two sizes. Small buckets are handy for little jobs like spot cleaning wall scuffs. Large buckets are best for big jobs like mopping floors.

CHAMOIS: A genuine leather chamois is essential for streak-free shining, as classic car aficionados well know. Keep one in the bathroom to wipe down shower doors and polish tile to a high shine. Keep another in the kitchen for polishing tile, stainless steel appliances and sinks, granite, and marble.

DUST BRUSHES AND CLOTHS: Dusting officially achieved its current status as a lost art in the 1960s, when a ragged remnant of a worn T-shirt and a can of chemical "dusting spray" replaced the traditional tools of the task. Our grandmothers knew better and kept a variety of cloths and brushes on hand for all of dusting's subtleties.

An old-fashioned horsehair counter brush is ideal for sweeping dust and dirt from polished surfaces such as granite, marble, stainless steel, and wood without scratching. A feather duster is perfect for chandeliers, figurines, mantel clocks, and other fragile valuables.

Unbleached flannel flip dusting cloths were favored in the grand houses of Victorian England. These versatile, washable cloths are designed to be folded, as you dust, into sixteen panels; when one panel gets dirty, you simply flip to the next. Silk cheesecloth—with its open, absorbent weave—is the fabric of choice for dusting with furniture cream or oil.

Avoid using diapers to dust and polish your fine wood furniture. Diapers that have been bleached will gradually wear away the patina of fine furniture.

MOPS: There have been lots of fancy advancements in mop design in recent years. But the fundamentals come down to two: the sponge mop and the dust mop.

The self-wringing sponge mop is designed for mopping floors and washing walls. There are several variations on wringing mechanisms; generally, those that must be operated down close to the mop head are less convenient than those that can be operated midway up the handle. When the sponge gets dirty, simply remove it and replace it.

For good wood floors, the dust mop is quieter than a vacuum, more effective than sweeping, and quicker than either of them. This mop is designed to be used dry. Shake outside or vacuum after using. Most have removable, machine-washable mop heads.

SQUEEGEES: Purchase two or three in a variety of blade lengths; they're indispensable for windows (except those with very small panes), glass shower doors, and large mirrors. Professionals swear by them.

TOOTHBRUSHES: Keep several inexpensive toothbrushes on hand for cleaning tight spots in the kitchen and bathroom. They're also handy for gently scrubbing small stains out of carpets and fabrics.

3. DECIDING WHERE TO BEGIN

You have everything you need: dusters, cleaners, mop, bucket, vacuum cleaner, and, of course, the messy house itself. Where do you start? Here are the five most common approaches:

Start at the top There's no use in polishing the table if you're going to dust the chandelier afterward—as soon as the dust falls from the chandelier, you'll have to clean the table again. A top-to-bottom approach keeps gravity from working against you. Start with the cobwebs on the ceiling, then do the light fixtures, then do the furniture, and end with vacuuming so you only have to do it once. If your home occupies more than one floor, consider starting on the top floor and finishing in the basement.

Go clockwise Or counterclockwise, if you prefer. The point is to get into the habit of always going in the same direction in every room so you don't overlook anything or repeat yourself.

Dry before wet The logic behind this approach is that you want to remove as much dirt as possible before you add anything that will turn dirt into mud—or before you rub something gritty into a surface that you're planning to shine. That's why our mothers taught us to sweep before mopping the floor, dust before polishing the furniture, and vacuum before shampooing the rug.

Difficult before easy If the sheer size of the job is keeping you from getting started, the best antidote may be to simply dive right in and tackle whatever looks like it's going to be the least fun and the most time-consuming. Once you get the most onerous task out of the way, you can coast through the rest of the room. But this approach doesn't work for everyone. If you're still stalled, read on.

Easy before difficult This approach utilizes the psychology of using small successes to build bigger ones. According to this reasoning, you should start with something small and achievable, like polishing a single candlestick. Your sense of accomplishment will inspire you to keep going and tackle ever bigger, more ambitious chores. If you're a procrastinator who doesn't respond well to the "difficult before easy" technique, give this a try.

TIMING

For generations, spring cleaning was timed to coincide with the arrival of warm weather so that doors and windows could be opened throughout the house. Fresh air was an absolute necessity, given how much dust an old-fashioned broom could stir up. Your mother or grandmother probably followed this tradition as well, to minimize the fumes from chemical cleansers and polishes.

Today you can commence your spring cleaning projects whenever you can find the time, even if it's too chilly to open the windows. Simply choose pleasantly scented, earth-friendly cleaners with plant-derived essential oils to match the mood of your household. Use lavender aromas to calm frazzled, overscheduled nerves. Try energizing citrus scents to counteract any lingering, late-winter lassitude. And be sure to use tools that allow you to pick up dust without spreading it around so that your efforts are truly a breath of fresh air.

ASIDE | SPRING CLEANING WITH MY MOTHER

My mother had nine children, and she didn't hesitate to put us to work when it was time for spring cleaning. She was a firm believer in washing walls, ceilings, and floors.

We used two buckets and a generous supply of clean cloths—never paper towels, because that was a waste of nature's resources. One bucket was for mild soap and water, and one bucket was for rinsing. Rinsing, in her opinion, was the most important part of the process. The slightest trace of residue completely spoiled the entire effort.

She would appoint a team of three kids: the lead soaper, the rinser, and the dryer. The most coveted job on the team was that of the rinser. Being the soaper was a much dirtier job, and if the rinser missed a spot, the dryer would usually catch it. The only drawback was being caught in the middle if the dryer thought that the soaper was moving too fast—or, worse, too slowly. Taunts would start flying, towels would start snapping, and my mother's efficient system would dissolve into giggles.

CLEANING WITH YOUR BRAIN ENGAGED

Spring cleaning is a great time to think about how to minimize your household's untidy habits. As you move through your house, look at every location where clutter congregates. You might start to feel frustrated—but don't give in. Try to maintain a state of cool, scientific detachment.

People who specialize in ergonomics spend their days observing how people behave. And then they design furnishings, spaces, and systems to accommodate those behaviors. Why? Because designing a chair that conforms to the ways people actually sit is far easier than trying to train people to sit in a way that conforms to the needs of the chair.

The same principles apply in your home. Perhaps the perennial pile of muddy shoes and boots by the back door isn't really a behavior problem. Instead, try viewing it as evidence that the hallway isn't equipped to accommodate the ways you actually use it. The solution could be as simple as putting a boot rack or mat by the door.

Other solutions can be just as easy to implement. Do you need a basket on the front hall table to catch stray papers such as mail and receipts? Would a different doormat do a better job of keeping dirt from being tracked in on the rug? Should you move the laundry hamper from the bedroom to the bathroom?

The purpose of this exercise is not to create a daunting to-do list that will keep you indoors until autumn. It's about brainstorming solutions that are appropriate to your life and proportionate to your resources. If you have a busy calendar, a tight budget, and a house full of kids, stick to ideas that are small and easy to implement. If you can afford to hire a cabinet maker or a closet organizer, then consider more ambitious projects.

To keep the process manageable, don't think in terms of "musts." Just think of "mights." Shift your thinking gently into problem-solving mode. Once you get the hang of it, it's actually fun. And if you tackle enough of your household clutter challenges, you could find yourself shaving hours off next year's spring cleaning schedule.

ASIDE | AROMATHERAPY FOR YOUR HOME

Aromatherapy is the use of plant-derived essential oils to enhance physical and psychological well-being. The benefits of flowers and herbs have long been available in cosmetic, bath, and body products. But only recently have these therapeutic properties been available in products formulated for the care of your home. Aromatherapy cleaners provide a pleasant change of pace from the harsh, chemical fragrances of many soaps, polishes, and detergents—as well as safe, effective alternatives for people who are concerned with the environmental effects of conventional cleaning products.

Scientists continue to confirm what traditional aromatherapy practitioners have always known about the powers and pleasures of plant, flower, and herb aromas—they make you feel as good as they smell. The scent of lavender produces calm and clarity. Citrus aromas create an alert, lively mood. Patchouli encourages contemplation and inspiration.

For most of us, being in the right mood for cleaning is a rare occurrence. Aromatherapy makes it far easier to attain this elusive mental state by providing a balance between the sensuous and the sensible. And its benefits linger in the air long after your work is done.

4. TIPS & TECHNIQUES

A generation ago, spring cleaning was achieved with harsh chemicals like chlorine bleach, ammonia, and synthetic fragrances. Today the art of keeping home draws from the wisdom of earlier, gentler times. Natural cleaners, made with plant-derived ingredients and readily available cleaning ingredients like baking soda, salt, lemons, and vinegar, are kinder to you, your belongings, and the planet. The following pages contain an A to Z listing of cleaning methods that you can use throughout your home. In addition to the topics in this chapter, you'll find room-by-room cleaning tips and techniques in Chapters 2 through 4. Chapter 4 includes specific information for cleaning walls, ceilings, countertops, appliances, and porcelain surfaces such as tubs and sinks.

BRASS: Use a paste made of equal parts salt and vinegar to polish brass. Salt and lemon juice also work—simply sprinkle salt onto the surface and rub with a halved lemon. A thin coat of paste wax will keep the tarnish from coming back. Antiques experts almost always advise against polishing old brass hardware; doing so can diminish the value of the furniture.

CARPET AND RUG STAINS: Blot fresh spills with a clean, white cloth or paper towel as soon as possible to soak up as much of the stain as possible. Apply a little club soda or cool water and blot again. If the stain remains, fill a spray bottle with water, add a couple drops of dish soap, and shake well. Spray the stain and gently work the lather into the spot with a toothbrush. Follow with clean water and blot firmly with a clean towel, absorbing as much water as possible. If any soap remains, rinse and blot again.

CHANDELIERS: A gentle dusting with a rooster feather duster is probably all your chandelier needs. You can also use the brush attachment on your vacuum cleaner extension, if it will reach that far safely. If your chandelier crystals have lost their sparkle, detach them—one section at a time so you can remember which ones go where—and wipe them gently with a soft cloth and a solution of half a cup of isopropyl alcohol diluted with two cups of water.

CHROME: Wipe with vinegar or polish with a sprinkle of baking soda on a damp cloth. Follow with a clean, damp cloth or chamois to remove any residue. Plain white toothpaste will also restore the shine—rub gently to avoid scratches.

CLOTHES, STORING: Always launder or dry-clean out-of-season clothes before storing them away. Moths are attracted to food stains, dirt, perspiration, and oils. Mothballs are noxious—anything that kills moths is not going to be particularly good for you either. Besides, they smell terrible. Traditional herbal moth repellents include ingredients such as cedar, eucalyptus, lavender, pennyroyal, rosemary, thyme, tobacco, and white pepper. Most are available at natural food stores. Prevention is the best defense; store your cashmere, silk, and wool garments in a securely built cedar chest or a sturdy, sealable storage container.

COPPER: A paste made of three parts salt to one part vinegar will restore tarnished copper to brightness. Check with your favorite antique dealer before polishing valuable vintage items—in many cases, polishing can actually lessen the value of a piece.

CURTAINS, DRAPERIES, AND SHADES: Unless your window treatments are spotted or stained, simply vacuum thoroughly on both sides with a brush attachment. Schedule professional cleanings sparingly to prolong the life of the fabrics. If you're planning to remove window treatments to take them to the cleaners, they'll be far more pleasant to handle if you vacuum them first.

Few window treatments are washable. For curtains that can handle the rigors of the washing machine, be sure to vacuum them beforehand to minimize the grime in the wash water.

DRAWERS: Wooden buffet, cabinet, and dresser drawers should be treated just like furniture exteriors. If more than a good dusting is called for, clean them with a clean cloth moistened with a small dab of wood furniture cream. To remedy a sticking drawer, rub a little candle wax on the drawer runners. This is a great way to use the last vestiges of your favorite aromatherapy candles, especially if the scent complements your drawer liners.

DUSTING: There is actually an art to this humble household task. The challenge is to remove dust, rather than just pushing it around or scattering it into the air. Use a thickly napped cloth, like flannel, or an open weave cloth, such as cheesecloth.

For wood furniture, moisten the cloth with a tiny dab of furniture cream. Start with oval strokes and end by dusting in the same direction as the grain. Dust intricately carved details by putting the cloth over the bristles of a soft toothbrush.

Creams and oils will leave residue on glass, ceramics, and stone. For these surfaces, use a clean cloth moistened with a very small amount of water so that the cloth is barely damp.

ELECTRONIC EQUIPMENT: It's not your imagination—these devices actually attract more dust by creating static electricity. Use the brush attachments of your vacuum cleaner to remove dust. Rub smudges with a little isopropyl alcohol. Never spray or pour anything directly on these machines. Moisten your cloth instead.

To clean dust, hair, and crumbs from between the keys of your computer keyboard, run the adhesive edge of a self-stick note between the rows. A really dirty keyboard may require four or five notes.

Televisions, stereos, and computers are delicate instruments. Always turn them off before cleaning.

FIREPLACES: Before you sweep the ashes from your fireplace, open the flue so that airborne particles will float up into the chimney, rather than out into the room. It's also a good idea to wear goggles for this task, especially if you wear contact lenses. Use a dustpan and brush to collect the ashes and deposit them gently into a bag. Close the bag immediately to contain any rising clouds of ash. Then use an art gum eraser (available at art supply stores) to remove any soot stains from the surrounding brickwork.

FLOORS, HARDWOOD: Sweep floor first, to remove any tracked-in dirt or grit. Then mop with a gentle, all-purpose cleaner diluted in a bucket of warm water. If you're out of cleaner, try weak tea: Pour a quart of water over two tea bags of plain, black tea. Let the solution cool to room temperature before using.

FLOORS, VINYL: Sweep thoroughly to remove any grit that will dull the shine. Scrub greasy trouble spots—by the stove, in the corners—with a halved lemon. Then mop with a gentle, all-purpose cleaner diluted in a bucket of hot water or dissolve a tablespoon of laundry borax in a bucket of hot water.

FURNITURE, CLEANING: Varnished wood furniture should be cleaned with a dab of furniture cream on a soft cloth. Cool black tea is also an effective cleaner for varnished wood. Clean with circular strokes.

To remove water rings from wood furniture, rub it with plain white toothpaste or apply vegetable oil mixed with enough salt to make a paste; let it sit for a couple of hours, then wipe clean.

Apply vegetable oil to scuffed table or chair legs and buff gently with fine-grade steel wool.

Clean a grimy yard sale treasure with a few drops of dish soap dissolved in warm water. Wash with a soft cloth, then rinse and dry immediately. A solution of white vinegar diluted with the same amount of water will clear away excess wax. Dry immediately with a clean towel.

FURNITURE, POLISHING: Furniture cream is formulated to both clean and polish furniture. You can also use petroleum jelly to restore the luster of old, dry wood.

MIRRORS: Never spray glass cleaner directly onto the edges of a mirror; the liquid can seep around the glass and onto the silvering, causing it to loosen and darken. Spray the cleaner onto your cloth instead. You can also use diluted vinegar to wash mirrors, though this option is not particularly fragrant.

PRECIOUS STONES: MARBLE AND GRANITE

MARBLE: Because this beautiful stone is highly porous, liquids soak in quickly, leaving possibly permanent stains. Marble is highly sensitive to the wrong cleaning products, so proceed with caution. Never use highly acidic cleaners such as vinegar, lemon juice, or ammonia. Wipe up all spills immediately with lukewarm water and a clean cloth. Shine with a chamois to reduce streaks. Once or twice a year, use a mild dish soap to remove soil. Rinse thoroughly and wipe dry.

Commercial sealers are available, but they require frequent reapplications. Some experts recommend sealing porous marble surfaces with a light coat of wax. Be sure to use a colorless wax. Avoid waxing white marble; it will yellow. A reliable local stone expert can help you remedy chips, cracks, and dullness.

GRANITE: Unlike marble, granite is relatively hard, nonporous, and hardy enough to withstand most cleaning liquids. Although experts agree that granite countertops require a sealant to repel water and stains, there is no consensus on precisely what that sealant should be. Some experts recommend a wax treatment, and others recommend a silicone seal. Whichever sealant you use, it's easy to test whether your counter is sealed properly. Simply pour a little water on it. If the seal is intact, the water will not penetrate and can be wiped off in a few seconds without leaving a damp spot.

If you have a penetrating rust stain, try the following poultice recipe. Deep or old stains may require more than one application. (Note: Never use this process on marble.)

Obtain oxalic acid from your hardware store or pharmacy. Mix it with kaolin or fuller's earth (types of powdered clay), unscented talc, or flour. Add just enough water to form a paste with the consistency of peanut butter. Wet the area with distilled water and apply a ¼-inch layer of this mixture to the stain, avoiding unstained surfaces. Cover the poultice with plastic wrap. Seal the edges with blue painter's tape. (Ordinary masking tape may leave a residue on the stone.) Use the tip of a sharp knife to poke a few holes in the plastic. Allow to dry completely, for twenty-four to forty-eight hours. Then scrape the poultice off the granite with a putty knife and wipe with a dry towel.

RUGS, ORIENTAL AND WOOL: If you want your rugs to have a long and beautiful life, be sure to treat them well. To give your rug a proper spring cleaning, start by moving all the furniture off the rug. Rotate the rug so that sun fading isn't concentrated on just one area. Check the padding underneath—synthetics will crumble over time and may abrade the rug backing or scratch your floors. Invest in a high quality, rubberized pad to protect your rug from wear. Run your hand over the pile to see the direction of the nap. You'll notice that the pile moves more smoothly in one direction than the others. Run the vacuum in that direction only, to prevent dirt from being ground into the rug. Use a gentle suction setting if your vacuum is adjustable. Otherwise use a floor attachment. Use special care on fringes, which will tangle and fray with overly vigorous vacuuming.

Some Oriental rug manufacturers recommend sweeping rugs with a broom to bring out the natural sheen of the wool. Always sweep in the direction of the pile.

RUGS, WASHING: If properly maintained with weekly vacuuming throughout the year, rugs will only need to be cleaned every three to five years. Room-size rugs should be professionally cleaned, but smaller rugs can be successfully cleaned at home. Vacuum the rug on both sides; then place it on a clean basement floor, driveway, or patio. Add a small amount of mild laundry soap or rug shampoo to a bucket of cool water. Dab a little soapy water on an inconspicuous corner to see if the dye will run. If it does, do not continue; consult a professional instead. If the dye is stable, lather the rug with a natural sea sponge, using smooth strokes in the direction of the pile. Lather the fringe by stroking it away from the rug edge.

Wring out the sponge and use it to press as much soap as you can from the rug. Then rinse well with a garden hose or in a utility sink. Lay the rug flat and press out as much water as possible by stroking the rug with a rubber squeegee in the direction of the pile. Lay the rug pile-side up on a dry surface. Once the pile side is completely dry, flip the rug over and allow the backing to dry thoroughly before returning the rug to its customary place.

SILVER: Remove tarnish by placing silver in a large pot or bowl with two teaspoons of salt, two teaspoons of baking soda, and a piece of aluminum foil. Cover with boiling water and wait three minutes. Remove silver, rinse, and dry well. Silver may also be polished with plain, white toothpaste—but rub very gently to avoid scratching, and rinse thoroughly or your next menu will need to be peppermint-compatible.

STAINLESS STEEL: Clean with baking soda and water. Rinse well and buff with a clean, soft cloth or a leather chamois.

TILE AND GROUT: If you run out of your favorite spray cleaner, use either vinegar or a loose paste of baking soda and water to clean. Do not combine! Rinse well and polish with a chamois. Scrub corners and grout with an old toothbrush. For stubborn grime, mix two parts baking soda with one part laundry borax. Scrub with a wet cloth and rinse well.

UPHOLSTERY, CLEANING: Vacuum fabric-covered furniture using the brush attachments on your vacuum hose extension. Spot clean stains with old-fashioned foamy shaving cream; rub gently and remove completely with a clean, damp cloth.

Leather upholstery should be cleaned with saddle, castile, or glycerin soap—and as little water as possible. Wipe with a barely damp cloth to remove soap residue and dry with a clean towel.

WALLS: A good ceiling-to-floor dusting with a long-handled dust mop is all you usually need for walls in the living room and bedroom. You can spot clean most scuffs and spatters with a little baking soda on a damp cloth or an art gum eraser from an art supply store. Use isopropyl alcohol to remove stray ink marks.

For rooms such as the kitchen and dining room, where food is prepared and served, an annual washing will remove visible grime, remove residues such as steam and smoke, and freshen the room. Washing the walls is also an essential step if your spring redecorating plans include adding a fresh coat of paint; a layer of grime, however slight, will prevent paint from adhering to your walls.

Use an all-purpose cleaner that is safe for painted walls. You'll also need a dust mop, two buckets, two wringable flat sponge mops, a plastic drop cloth, and something to keep the cloth in position while you're working, such as a low-adhesive painter's tape or a few small items that can serve as weights. Follow these steps:

1. Move furniture to the center of the room. Take down any mirrors or artwork.

2. Dust ceilings and walls.

3. Pick a wall to start with and position your drop cloth on the floor, right up against the edge. Apply tape or weights to keep it in place.

4. Mix one bucket with cleaner and warm water, according to package directions. Fill the other bucket with clean water for rinsing.

5. Assign one mop to the wash bucket and one to the rinse bucket. If your mops are identical, put a piece of tape or string on one handle so you can tell them apart.

6. Wring out the wash bucket mop so that it's just damp and clean the wall with gentle, smooth vertical strokes, from top to bottom. When you've cleaned a three-foot-wide section, switch to the rinse mop, which should also be wrung to minimize dripping. Rinse each section before moving to the next to prevent cleanser residue from drying on the walls.

7. Empty and refill your buckets when the water gets dirty. Try to finish a wall completely before you take a break, to avoid noticeable streaks.

8. When you finish a wall, move your drop cloth to the next wall and continue to the next until all are clean. Then take a moment to admire how much brighter and fresher the room seems to be!

WINDOWS: Washing windows is the quintessential spring cleaning chore: It's the kind of task you'd never dream of doing on a weekly basis; it requires a considerable amount of time; and it repays your efforts with especially satisfying results. Nothing makes a room sparkle quite like freshly washed windows. The best weather for doing windows is warm, dry, and overcast. Strong sunlight will cause the cleaner to dry quickly, leaving streaks on the glass.

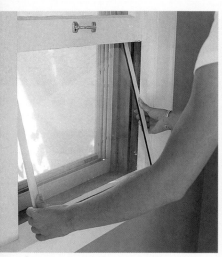

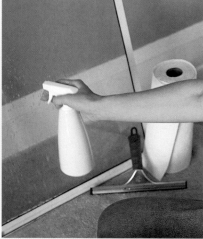

1. Spread the bath towel on the floor under the window. Open the window; slide the storm window and screen out and into the room. Set the screen aside. (See page 34 for screen cleaning.)

2. Prop the lower edge of the storm window on the towel. Spray one side with cleaner. Wipe with the squeegee. Use a paper towel to wipe the squeegee dry between strokes. When you finish one side, flip the window and do the other.

3. Clean the inside of the window glass just like the storm window. To minimize streaks, alternate the direction of your squeegee so that you wipe the inside of the glass horizontally and outside vertically.

But window cleaning is such a big chore—and such an important part of your spring cleaning ritual—that it makes sense to schedule it for a time that fits into your schedule. And there's no rule that says you have to do it all at once. You can do the insides on one day and the outsides on the next. Do a room at a time, if you like. Start on the inside with a bottle of window cleaner, a roll of paper towels, an old bath towel, and a squeegee. Then follow these steps.

4. Spray the sill with cleaner and wipe clean with a paper towel (or two—sills can get really dirty).

5. Go outside and clean the outside of the window glass.

6. Reinstall the screen and storm window.

WINDOW SCREENS: If you want your clean windows to stay clean for as long as possible, you need to clean your screens. Window screens collect a surprising amount of grime, most of which you won't see until it makes its way onto your windows, courtesy of the wind and rain.

The easiest way to clean screens is outdoors with a garden hose and a scrub brush. Just spray each screen with the hose, scrub with the brush, and spray again. Leave them propped against a porch or chair to dry in the sun.

If you're an apartment dweller without access to a garden hose and a backyard, there are two methods you can use to clean screens indoors.

1. Rest the bottom edge of the screen on the floor on an old towel. Spot clean any obvious crud (such as bird dirt) with a scrub brush and a squirt of window cleaner. Then hold an old, lint-free towel flat against one side of the screen and vacuum with the brush attachment of your vacuum cleaner. Keep moving the towel to correspond with the position of the vacuum brush so that it is always supporting the area of the screen you are vacuuming. When you have finished one side, flip the towel over and clean the other side the same way.

2. If you have access to a basement laundry tub, you can wash all but the largest screens there. Fill the tub with about six inches of hot water and a squirt of all-purpose cleaner. Use a scrub brush to remove the grime. Rinse thoroughly—soap residue will give dirt something to stick to. Allow to dry completely before installing the screen back into the window frame.

WOODWORK: Wherever there are doorways and windowsills, there are bound to be fingerprints and smudges. If you find yourself with a spare five minutes, put a dab of all-purpose cleaner on a damp cloth and wipe away any grime from areas surrounding light switches, doorknobs, cabinet pulls, and window hardware. Check the woodwork around the doorways, too—you're likely to find additional smudges at about shoulder height, where people tend to touch as they enter or leave a room.

Although daily and weekly maintenance is the first line of defense against hair, dander, and dirty paw prints, attending to our four-legged friends is an integral part of spring cleaning. Thorough vacuuming is essential. Mopping floors and shampooing rugs will keep telltale pet odors to a minimum. Pay special attention to their favorite places. Launder their bedding and wash their food and water dishes. Take apart litter boxes to wash and dry them thoroughly. Sending your animals to the groomers while you are spring cleaning will keep them out of your way while you're working—and postpone the inevitable return of hair and dander once you're done.

Our cats are named Prancer (a gray, bossy tabby) and Clara (a big, out-of-shape flirt), and they love sneaking into open drawers, closets, and even the dryer. Without a doubt, they are the messiest members of our household!

TECHNIQUE | HOW TO BEAT A RUG

Before electricity and vacuum cleaners, dusty rugs were dragged outside, hung over a line, and beaten clean with a rug beater, a long-handled tool with a large, looped, wire head. Old-fashioned rug beaters were built to withstand years of vigorous use, so you can often find perfectly workable versions in antique stores. If you don't have a well-stocked antique store nearby, an old tennis racquet works just as well.

For small rugs that tend to get drawn up into the vacuum cleaner, beating is actually easier. Give it a try on a dry, breezy day. Fold the rug lengthwise over the line, inside out. Stand upwind of the rug and beat downwind—otherwise, you'll simply be transferring the dirt from your rug to your clothing. Give it five to ten good, firm strokes. Flip the rug on the line so the side you've just beaten is now downwind. Beat again. Then turn the rug right-side out and beat both halves again. Never shake or beat a rag rug—you'll snap the warp threads. Vacuum it thoroughly instead.

2

THE PUBLIC SPACES

Task-by-task guidelines for the rooms where you welcome and entertain your family and friends.

We should gain more by letting ourselves be seen such as we are,
than by attempting to appear what we are not.

— FRANÇOIS DE LA ROCHEFOUCAULD

IF YOUR TIME IS LIMITED BECAUSE YOUR SOCIAL CALENDAR is brimming with springtime entertaining plans, focus your efforts on the places where you welcome your friends: the entryway, living room, and dining room.

Even though you'll be focusing on the public spaces of your home, remember that spring cleaning is about taking care of yourself, not polishing an unrealistic image to present to others. The notion of home care as self care is the opposite of perfectionism— that tyrannical yardstick that makes you feel as though you can never measure up.

Your sparkling house will never be truly welcoming if you are too tired and stressed to enjoy your guests. Always give yourself permission to be human. And let the little things slide once in a while.

1. THE ENTRYWAY

The entryway is a great place to begin your spring cleaning efforts. It's small, so that a relatively small investment of time and effort will provide you with a wonderful sense of accomplishment. And it's one of the most public areas of your home, so you'll make a great first impression on your visitors.

Entry areas tend to accumulate the things we bring into our homes from the outside: mail, briefcases, gym bags, shopping bags, boots, etc. The floors get the worst of tracked-in dirt.

Start by making a list of everything you can see that needs cleaning. Begin your appraisal at the ceiling and work your way down to the floor. You can tailor the following master list to the specifics of your space.

MASTER LIST | ENTRYWAY

Remove cobwebs in corners

Dust light fixtures

Replace burned-out bulbs

Wash windows

Wash walls

Wipe woodwork

Dust framed artwork

Clean mirrors

Dust and polish architectural details (such as stair railings)

Declutter tables and other surfaces

Polish furniture

Shake out doormat

Sweep and mop floor

After you identify the areas of your entryway that need cleaning, think about what kinds of tools and supplies you need for each task. Then estimate how much time you think you'll need. Notations for the items on your list might look like this.

SAMPLE PLAN | ENTRYWAY = 1 HOUR, 58 MINUTES

TASK	TOOLS ($ = need to buy)	TIME
Remove cobwebs in corners	Vacuum cleaner with hose extension	10 min
Dust light fixtures	Long-handled duster	2 min
Replace lightbulbs	Lightbulbs ($)	5 min
Clean out coat closet	Trash bags	60 min
Shake out doormat		1 min
Sweep floor	Broom, dustpan	10 min
Mop floor	Mop, bucket, cleaner ($)	30 min

Once you have identified your tasks, tools, and time requirements, refer to Chapter 1, pages 23–34, for specifics on cleaning mirrors, walls, woodwork, and more. Then consult your calendar and schedule the tasks you want to do first.

CELEBRATE A JOB WELL DONE :: *Reward yourself with an aromatherapy candle or two for your freshly cleaned entryway. Even when they're not burning, they'll make a fragrant first impression on visitors.*

2. THE LIVING ROOM

Generations ago, the living room was the showcase of the household, a place where guests were invited to make themselves at home, surrounded by the family's most valuable furnishings and treasures. In an age where formal entertaining was the fashion, this room was reserved for socializing of the highest standard.

Today, as our entertaining rituals have relaxed, the living room comes to life as a full-fledged, everyday member of the household. Now that the living room is more livable, it's much more likely to suffer from spills on the rug and soot on the fireplace.

Pick up your notebook and examine your living room from ceiling to floor. Or check the elements of your room against the master list below.

MASTER LIST | LIVING ROOM

Remove cobwebs in corners	Dust books and bookcases	Spot clean rug
Dust artwork	Polish candlesticks	Steam clean carpet
Vacuum window treatments	Polish mantel	Vacuum behind and beneath furniture
Wash windows	Polish furniture	
Dust lamps	Clean fireplace and hearth	Polish wood floor

Once you've decided on a plan for the room, refer to the alphabetical listing of cleaning tips in Chapter 1, pages 23–34, for advice about polishing marble, cleaning the fireplace, and more. Your plan might look like this.

SAMPLE PLAN | LIVING ROOM = 2 HOURS, 10 MINUTES

TASK	TOOLS ($ = need to buy)	TIME
Remove cobwebs in corners	Vacuum cleaner with hose extension	10 min
Dust lamps	Dust cloth	20 min
Vacuum window treatments	Vacuum cleaner with hose extension	15 min
Polish marble mantel	Baking soda, lemon juice	15 min
Polish furniture	Wood cream ($), marble polish ($)	30 min
Spot clean rug	Dish soap, bucket, cloth, toothbrush	10 min
Clean fireplace and hearth	Vinegar, art gum eraser, dustpan, brush	20 min
Vacuum	Vacuum cleaner	10 min

CELEBRATE A JOB WELL DONE :: *Add life to your living room and treat yourself to a beautiful bouquet of fresh peonies or lilacs.*

THE TIDY LIBRARY: CARING FOR BOOKS AND BOOKCASES

Depending on how much time you have—and how many books—this is a job that can take ten minutes or an entire afternoon. To clean your bookcases quickly, simply use the small brush attachment on your vacuum cleaner. Clean the tops of the books, then the spines. Run the brush along the edge of the shelf. Then take four or five books from the center of each section so you can reach behind the rest and vacuum the top, bottom, and back of the shelf. Slide the remaining books to one side, then the other, so you can dust the sides of the bookshelf. Then replace the books you removed.

If you have more time, cleaning your bookcases lovingly is a wonderful way to spend a rainy afternoon. Start by making yourself a cup of tea. Place a saucer over the top of your teacup to protect it from dust. Take out one book at a time and dust it on all sides with the brush from your vacuum cleaner. Once you empty each section, vacuum the interior thoroughly. Polish the wood with a soft cloth and a small dab of furniture cream. Then return the books to the shelves, restoring any lapses in alphabetical order. If you have more books than shelves, think about selecting a few titles to give away. Schools, libraries, and churches often schedule book sales in the spring where you can help your outgrown books to find appreciative new owners.

You will get distracted frequently, as you page through old favorites. That's okay. Make yourself another cup of tea.

3. THE DINING ROOM

The dining room is rich with tradition. Its sparkling chandelier, delicate china, and gleaming candlesticks evoke memories of holiday gatherings, elegant dinner parties, and cherished family celebrations.

If you only use your dining room for special occasions (and occasional stints as a home office) it might not need much more than a good, thorough dusting and vacuuming. But even seldom-used dining rooms are worth a closer look, especially if you'll be entertaining this spring.

Eye the room from top to bottom with notebook and pen in hand. You can adapt this master list to the needs of your dining room.

MASTER LIST | DINING ROOM

Remove cobwebs in corners	Wash windows	Spot clean rug
Dust chandelier	Polish candlesticks	Steam clean carpet
Dust artwork	Polish silver	Vacuum behind and beneath furniture
Vacuum window treatments	Polish furniture	

Once you identify the areas of your dining room that need cleaning, notations for the items on your list might look like this.

SAMPLE PLAN | DINING ROOM = 1 HOUR, 45 MINUTES

TASK	TOOLS ($ = need to buy)	TIME
Remove cobwebs in corners	Vacuum cleaner with hose extension	10 min
Clean chandelier	Isopropyl alcohol ($), clean cloths	20 min
Vacuum window treatments	Vacuum cleaner with hose extension	15 min
Polish brass candlesticks	Vinegar, salt, sponge	10 min
Polish furniture	Wood cream ($)	30 min
Spot clean rug	Dish soap, bucket, cloth, toothbrush	10 min
Vacuum	Vacuum cleaner	10 min

See Chapter 1, pages 23 and 30, for tips on polishing brass and silver. Then consult your calendar, gather your tools, and think about how wonderful it will be to have your dining room ready for all the special occasions of the coming season.

CELEBRATE A JOB WELL DONE :: *Accessorize your gleaming dining room by placing a beautiful crystal bowl filled with fresh fruit on the table.*

4. THE PORCH

If the weather is fine and the great outdoors is beckoning, you don't have to abandon your spring cleaning plan—just take it outside and get your porch ready for a season of relaxing.

Bring out your notebook and start with a top-to-bottom assessment or use the master list below as a checklist.

MASTER LIST | PORCH

Remove cobwebs in corners	Wipe down furniture	Mop floor
Clean porch screens	Sweep floor	

After you review the cleaning needs of your porch, your plan might look like this:

SAMPLE PLAN | PORCH = 2 HOURS, 20 MINUTES

TASK	TOOLS ($ = need to buy)	TIME
Remove cobwebs in corners	Long-handled broom	10 min
Clean screens	All-purpose cleaner, bucket, scrub brush	60 min
Wipe down furniture	All-purpose cleaner, bucket, cloth	30 min
Sweep floor and steps	Broom	10 min
Mop floor	Mop, bucket, all-purpose cleaner	30 min

After you determine a plan for your porch, see listings in Chapter 1, pages 32–34, to find out how to clean screens and windows. Then check the weather forecast, gather your supplies, and get started.

Keep an eye out for evidence of uninvited insects as you're cleaning your porch. Check the ceiling corners for wasp nests. Tidy little piles of sawdust on the floor may indicate that your porch is hosting a colony of carpenter ants. Ask the experts at your neighborhood hardware store for advice about the safest way to evict these pests.

CELEBRATE A JOB WELL DONE :: *Every spring we open up our three-season porch and discover musty air, spiderwebs, buggy corners, forgotten magazines, and half-burned candles. We usually spend the first warm Friday night cleaning our porch from top to bottom. As soon as our neighbors see us trundling our well-worn white wicker furniture out the back porch door, they start counting down. They know that the minute the job is done, it's officially gin & tonic season at our house. In fact, one friend paces up and down the alley to make sure he doesn't miss the first round.*

Before we pick up our brooms, we make sure the gin and glasses are in the freezer, the limes and tonic are well chilled, and we're stocked with plenty of ice.

THE OFFICIAL NASSIF GIN & TONIC RECIPE

1. Fill frosted glasses with ice

2. Squeeze a big lime wedge over the ice and drop it into the glass

3. Add one to two fingers of gin

4. Fill with tonic

5. Turn on Ella Fitzgerald

6. Toast your friends and enjoy

3

THE PRIVATE SPACES

Going behind closed doors to clean the places you call your own.

Lose not the advantage of solitude, and the society of thyself.
— SIR THOMAS BROWNE

PRIVATE SPACE IS WHAT DISTINGUISHES A HOME FROM a showroom. Every home needs a place behind the scenes where you can leave things out, wander around half-undressed, unwind, recharge, and hide things away.

When time is tight, it's tempting to overlook your bedroom and closets. But since they are the most personal spaces in your home, giving them a good spring cleaning is truly a gift to yourself.

1. THE BEDROOM

The ideal bedroom is a sanctuary, your softly upholstered refuge from a world where you have to be clean, pressed, punctual, and ready for whatever comes your way. Privacy is the bedroom's greatest strength—and its greatest weakness.

You don't have to clean the bedroom if you're having company over for dinner. So you don't. It's so much easier to just close the door. And leave it that way. As long as your eyes are closed and the lights are out, why should it matter that you haven't dusted in a month?

The bedroom is like the quiet middle child of the family: It never makes any demands or gives you a moment's trouble until it disappears for a week and comes back with a spouse named Spike.

Your bedroom probably won't run away from home, but if neglected for long, it will develop some scary characteristics. That overlooked pile of laundry will turn your only clean shirt into a crumpled rag on a morning when you don't have time to iron. That thick layer of dust will aggravate allergies you didn't even know you had.

Because a vigorous cleaning can stir up dust, try to schedule your bedroom cleaning for a day when you can open all the windows.

Take up your notebook and evaluate your bedroom from ceiling to floor. Or check the elements of your room against the master list below.

MASTER LIST | BEDROOM

Remove cobwebs in corners	Declutter surfaces	Collect unneeded clothing for charity donations
Dust artwork	Polish furniture	Spot clean rug
Vacuum window treatments	Flip the mattress	
Wash windows	Change and launder bedding	Vacuum behind and beneath furniture
Dust lamps	Clean out dresser drawers	

After you review the cleaning needs of your bedroom, your plan might look like this:

SAMPLE PLAN | BEDROOM = 2 HOURS, 5 MINUTES

TASK	TOOLS ($ = need to buy)	TIME
Remove cobwebs in corners	Vacuum cleaner with hose extension	10 min
Dust lamps	Dust cloth	20 min
Vacuum window treatments	Vacuum cleaner with hose extension	15 min
Polish furniture	Wood cream	30 min
Clean and reline dresser drawers	Dust cloth, drawer liners ($)	20 min
Mop wood floors	Floor-friendly cleaner, mop, bucket	30 min

THE BEDSIDE TABLE

Our bedroom is where we hide from the world to read books, watch TV, and snuggle with our children. So our bedside tables are part medicine chest, part office, and part living room end table, equipped with everything from coasters for beverages to foot balm for tired feet.

Rather than trying to control the inevitable clutter, we've decided to embrace it. Having everything we need within arm's reach of the bed is the ultimate luxury. So we stock our bedside tables with all kinds of things that make us feel good at the end of a long day.

- :: A drawer full of writing implements, memo pads, sticky notes to mark books, and mints
- :: Moistened hand wipes to remove newspaper ink and traces of midnight snacks
- :: Photos of our girls when they were little
- :: Coasters for iced tea and wineglasses
- :: Tissues for crying at sappy old movies
- :: Hand lotion and foot balm
- :: Basket for magazines and newspapers
- :: Stacks of favorite books, including short stories, novellas, and poetry for nights when we need to read just a little bit before snoozing
- :: A small, decorative dish to hold jewelry

BRAINSTORM A BETTER BEDROOM

Because sleeping well is so important to your overall quality of life, use your spring cleaning time to make a wish list of bedroom improvement projects. If you're always waking up with a stuffy nose, consider getting allergen-proof covers for your mattress and pillows. Does the light from the street keep you awake? Think about installing light-blocking window shades. If your morning dressing routine has you leaping over the bed as you travel back and forth between your closet and your dresser, try rearranging the furniture.

CELEBRATE A JOB WELL DONE :: *A new pillow can make a world of difference in the quality of your sleep. Treat yourself—and rediscover what it's like to wake up in the morning without that little crick in your neck. Try a new shape: Pillows are now specially designed to accommodate your preferred back, side, or stomach sleeping style.*

2. CLOSETS

Even though closets are hidden behind closed doors, cleaning a closet is an immensely satisfying way to create order from chaos. Cleaning a closet is fairly straightforward. Spend a few minutes with your notebook and look over your closet from top to bottom. If you can't see the coats for the clutter, use the following master list to get started.

MASTER LIST | CLOSET

Empty the closet	Dust and wipe hanging rod and unused hangers	Identify unneeded items for charity donations
Remove cobwebs in corners	Replace shelf liner paper	Put coats, woolens, and other winter clothes in storage
Dust and wipe shelves	Wash walls	
Vacuum floor		

After reviewing and identifying what your closet needs, your plan might look like this:

SAMPLE PLAN | CLOSET = 1 HOUR, 5 MINUTES

TASK	TOOLS ($ = need to buy)	TIME
Remove cobwebs in corners	Vacuum cleaner with hose extension	10 min
Wash walls	All-purpose cleaner, bucket, sponge, mop	20 min
Collect giveaway goods	Big trash bags	30 min
Vacuum floor	Vacuum cleaner	5 min

PERFECT PITCHING

When it comes to determining what to keep and what to pitch, people either decide with their heads or their hearts. People who decide with their heads use ruthlessly logical criteria to determine whether an item should stay or go. These are the people who follow the "Have you worn it or used it in a year?" rule. It's a pretty good rule—until you give away something only to regret it later.

People who decide with their hearts almost never throw anything out. They want to keep their outgrown jeans in case they lose ten pounds. They want to keep the expensive silk blouse in case shoulder pads come back into fashion. They want to keep the prom dress, and the wedding dress, and the christening gown, because sentimental value is indeed valuable. The only problem with this approach is that they also want to buy new things, but they don't have any place to put them.

Between the two extremes is a third possibility. You can compromise your way to a cleaner closet. This approach requires a bit of creativity: Challenge yourself to think of either a better way to store the item or a better way to think about giving it up.

CELEBRATE A JOB WELL DONE :: *Keep your closet smelling fresh by storing fragrant soaps or candles on the top shelf. Or invest in some cedar hangers.*

4

THE PRACTICAL PLACES

Working on the hardest-working rooms in your home: the kitchen, bathroom, laundry room, and basement.

I long to accomplish a great and noble task, but it is my chief duty
to accomplish small tasks as if they were noble.
— HELEN KELLER

THE HARDEST WORKING ROOMS OF YOUR HOME—

the kitchen, bathroom, laundry room, and basement—have been under siege in recent years. The sensible soap-and-water regimens of our grandmothers have been jettisoned in favor of veritable armies of antibacterial and antiviral products. Consumers who have been trained to fear germs now spend millions of dollars each year on household germ warfare.

Unfortunately, the germs are winning. Scientists now believe that our growing dependence on these products, like our widespread use of antibiotic medications, is actually creating more resistant strains of bacteria and viruses. Germs learn to adapt to survive—and they're adapting far more quickly than our immune systems can respond. If we don't give ourselves a chance to develop immunity to lesser germs, we may become more vulnerable to the new "super bugs."

The best defense is a back-to-basics approach. Traditional sanitary practices—washing with the hottest water possible, keeping sponges and rags clean and dry, and enforcing a sensible hand-washing policy—will go a long way toward keeping your household healthy. Because the kitchen and bathroom pose special cleaning challenges, the following pages include specific tips and techniques for these hardworking rooms.

1. THE KITCHEN

If you believe that the way to tackle a large-scale job like spring cleaning is to get the biggest, most difficult part out of the way first, then you'll probably want to start with the kitchen. The kitchen is the hive of activity in most homes. It's also where you'll find the many cleaning challenges of food preparation and storage.

Grab your notebook and pen and make a list of everything you can see that needs cleaning, using the master list below as a guide.

MASTER LIST | KITCHEN

Remove cobwebs in corners

Spot clean ceiling food stains

Dust light fixtures

Wash windows

Empty and wipe down cabinet and drawer interiors

Gather unneeded canned goods for local food bank

Wipe cabinet doors

Weed out unused pots, pans, and appliances to give away

Wash walls

Clean refrigerator

Clean oven

Declutter countertops and other surfaces

Clean microwave interior

Move all countertop appliances to clean beneath them

Wipe spills and spots from appliances

Wipe down table and chairs

Clean rug

Sweep and scrub floor

If you were to tackle this entire list from top to bottom, it would easily take the whole weekend. But don't get discouraged—you probably don't have to do it all. Consider how much time you have, and how your kitchen has been maintained throughout the year, to determine which aspects of your kitchen need attention. Once you identify your tasks, a more manageable kitchen plan might look like this.

SAMPLE PLAN | KITCHEN = 3 HOURS, 42 MINUTES

TASK	TOOLS ($ = need to buy)	TIME
Spot clean ceiling and wall spatters	Ladder, spray cleaner, cloth	30 min
Dust light fixtures	Long-handled duster	2 min
Clean all cabinet exterior doors and select cabinet interiors	Spray cleaner, cloth	45 min
Clean refrigerator	Baking soda ($), clean cloths, small bucket	60 min
Clean oven	Baking soda ($), sponge	45 min
Wipe countertops	Spray cleaner, cloth	10 min
Sweep and scrub floor	Broom, mop, scrub brush, bucket, cleaner	30 min

Appliances Use rubbing alcohol to clean and shine the exteriors of small kitchen appliances. (Alcohol fumes are highly flammable. Make sure all your gas stove burners are turned off.)

Butcher block counters Sanding and re-oiling your butcher block surfaces is a messy, dusty job. But if you're willing to commit to the time required—anywhere from ninety minutes to two hours, depending on the size of your kitchen—the results are positively rejuvenating.

Start by removing all items from the counter. Tape plastic drop cloths or newspaper over any open shelving to protect their contents from dust.

Use a palm sander or an electric hand sander. With the newer rotary vibrating models, the sandpaper simply pops on with Velcro. Use fine-grade sandpaper and sand along the grain to remove stains and grease spots. Change the sandpaper as soon as it becomes coated with dirt. Don't overlook the front edges and backsplashes. For corners the sander can't reach, sand by hand with grade 000 steel wool.

Once all stains and spots are gone, use a vacuum cleaner with a brush attachment to remove excess dust. Then wipe the counters with a slightly damp cloth or a tack cloth (a slightly sticky cloth available at hardware stores) to remove every last trace of dust.

To finish, apply butcher block oil (a food-safe, nontoxic mineral oil) liberally with a brush or clean cloth. Allow to penetrate for five minutes. Rub well, first against the grain, then along the grain for a rich patina.

Ceilings Unless you have very high ceilings or you never cook, you'll probably notice a few spots of sauce and smoke on your kitchen ceiling from time to time. If your spot cleaning efforts leave you with a couple of obviously clean patches that don't match the rest of the ceiling, you may want to clean the whole thing.

Ceiling grime is a natural by-product of cooking. Grease and food particles travel upward on the warmth of steam and smoke. Even washing dishes—by hand or machine—creates steam that can mark your ceilings over time.

Smooth, painted ceilings are the easiest to clean. Textured, spray finishes (also known as "popcorn" ceilings) cannot be cleaned without dislodging chunks of the finish. Simply dust or vacuum these ceilings thoroughly. If you have a suspended ceiling where square or rectangular panels are held in place on a lightweight metal grid, simply replace any stained panels with new ones. Replacement panels, available at home improvement stores, are usually inexpensive and easy to install.

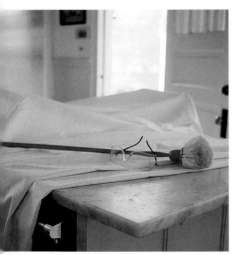

1. Pick a corner to start with and drape the drop cloth over the counters, appliances, and furnishings beneath it. Put on your goggles to protect your eyes and dust the area with your dust mop.

2. Mix one bucket with cleaner and warm water. Fill the other bucket with clean water for rinsing. Assign one mop to the wash bucket and one to the rinse bucket. If your mops are identical, put a piece of tape or string on one handle so you can tell them apart.

3. Wring out the wash bucket mop so that it's barely damp and mop the ceiling with gentle, smooth strokes.

Use an all-purpose cleaner that is safe for painted walls. You'll also need a dust mop, two buckets, two wringable flat sponge mops, a plastic drop cloth, and something to keep the cloth in position while you're working, such as a low-adhesive painter's tape or a few small items that can serve as weights. Once you have all your supplies, follow these steps.

4. Approach corners gently—if you bang the mop too close to the edge, you'll create streaks on the wall. Hold the mop at an angle, rather than standing directly underneath it, so that the wash water won't drip on you.

5. When you've cleaned a three-foot-wide section, switch to the rinse mop, which should also be well wrung to minimize dripping. Rinse each section before moving to the next to prevent cleanser residue from drying in streaks on the ceiling.

6. Empty and refill your buckets if the water gets dirty. When you finish one section, move your drop cloth to the next part of the room and continue until the whole ceiling is clean.

Cupboards and drawers Kitchen drawers and cupboards can accumulate a surprising amount of crumbs and spills. Empty them first. Then vacuum thoroughly to remove dust and crumbs. Use a paste of baking soda and water to clean and deodorize. Remove the cleaner with a clean, damp cloth and leave the drawer open and empty until completely dry.

Take a few minutes to sort through things before you put them back. Spring cleaning is the perfect opportunity to get rid of rusty can openers, crumbling rubber spatulas, and anything else that's past its prime. For herbs, spices, and vitamins, pitch anything that's more than a year old. Check expiration or "use by" dates. And make a list of things you need to replace.

Dishwasher To remove detergent residue and hard water deposits from your dishwasher, pour two cups of white vinegar into an otherwise empty dishwasher. Then close and run through a normal wash and rinse cycle.

Garbage disposal Cut the rind of one lemon into large chunks and feed into the disposal. Turn on the tap and run the disposal for several seconds. (Use the juice to clean your microwave; see below.)

Microwave To loosen cooked-on food from the interior of your microwave oven, fill a bowl with a cup of water and the juice of one lemon. Microwave on high for three to four minutes, or until water comes to a full boil and creates steam. Leave the door closed for several minutes so that the steam can penetrate. Clean the interior with a cloth and hot, soapy water. Then wipe with a clean, damp cloth and leave the door open until the interior is completely dry.

Nooks and crannies   Grime happens in the most inconvenient places—such as the grooves on your appliances, the corners of your countertops, and the edges of your sink. To scrub these hard-to-clean kitchen crevices, wrap a cleaning cloth firmly around the blade of an old butter knife. Spray the area with cleaner and slide the wrapped knife blade along the crevice to remove stubborn, sticky dirt.

Oven cleaning   If you have a self-cleaning oven, this task couldn't be easier. Simply lock the oven door and turn the dial to self-clean. The grease and grime is simply vaporized by the high heat. Remember to open the windows and follow the advice of your oven's manufacturer. Avoid cleaning your oven right before a dinner party; the process sometimes creates an odd mechanical smell that will not complement your roast.

You don't need a harsh oven cleaner if you have a box of baking soda. Soda is a natural plant ash—highly absorbent, highly alkaline, and highly amenable to bonding with grease. Sprinkle the bottom of the oven with baking soda to cover completely. Spritz with water until very damp. Allow to set overnight. Then simply open up and scoop up the baking soda and grime. Make sure you wipe the oven several times with a clean, moist cloth to remove all traces of soda and grease.

Refrigerator   Set aside at least an hour for this time-consuming task.

1. Turn the refrigerator off. Throw away anything that's past its prime. Store all remaining food in coolers.

2. Remove all shelves and bins. Wash in dish soap and water; allow to dry completely.

3. Wash the interior with baking soda and water. Rinse and dry completely.

4. Clean seals and gaskets with vinegar, scrubbing any mildew stains with a toothbrush.

5. Replace shelves and bins. Turn refrigerator back on.

6. Put the food back.

Stove cooktops   If you have an electric stove with coil burners, lift the coils gently and remove the drip pans underneath. Soak the pans in a sink full of hot, soapy water and scrub with a nonabrasive sponge or cloth. Dry thoroughly before putting them back.

For gas stoves, remove the metal burner grates and soak them in hot, sudsy water. Any stubborn residue can be scrubbed with steel wool. Clean around the burners with baking soda and water. A toothbrush will help you clean the crevices. Make sure burner grates are completely dry before putting them back on the burners.

Smooth glass and ceramic surfaces can be cleaned with a sprinkle of baking soda on a moist, soft cloth. Follow by wiping with a clean, damp cloth to remove any residue.

CELEBRATE A JOB WELL DONE :: *Complement your sparkling clean kitchen with a bevy of your favorite fresh herbs, like lavender or rosemary, planted in painted terra-cotta pots.*

2. THE BATHROOM

After the kitchen, the bathroom is probably the most frequently used room in your home. And, like your kitchen, it probably gets plenty of cleaning attention throughout the year. Even so, spring cleaning is a great time to catch up on neglected bathroom chores.

Bring your notebook and pen and make a list of everything you can see that needs cleaning. Use the master list below for ideas.

MASTER LIST | BATHROOM

Remove cobwebs in corners	Wash mirrors	Clean tile grout
Dust light fixtures	Empty and wipe down cabinet and drawer interiors	Launder shower curtain
Remove hard water residue from showerhead	Wipe cabinet doors	Scrub toilet
Wash windows	Declutter countertops and other surfaces	Scrub tub
Wash walls		Sweep floor
	Clean countertops and sink	Scrub floor

Think about how much time you want to spend, and how you have maintained your bathroom throughout the year, to identify which elements of your bathroom need the most attention.

Once you identify your tasks and your tools, your complete plan might look like this.

SAMPLE PLAN | BATHROOM = 2 HOURS, 42 MINUTES

TASK	TOOLS ($ = need to buy)	TIME
Remove cobwebs	Broom	10 min
Remove residue from showerhead	Vinegar	5 min
Clean cabinets and drawers	Spray cleaner, cloth	45 min
Wipe mirrors	Glass cleaner, cloth or paper towels	2 min
Launder shower curtain	Laundry soap, washing machine	45 min
Wipe countertops and sink	Spray cleaner, cloth	10 min
Scrub tub	Vinegar or baking soda, sponge	5 min
Scrub toilet	Toilet cleaner, brush, spray cleaner, cloth	10 min
Sweep and scrub floor	Broom, mop, scrub brush, bucket, cleaner	30 min

Bathroom stains For limestone, rust, and hard water residues, dilute white vinegar with an equal amount of water. Apply with an old toothbrush and scrub. Be sure to rinse thoroughly.

Mildew is a dark, spotty fungus that thrives in damp conditions. It is extremely difficult to treat with nonnoxious chemicals. Very mild cases may respond to applications of undiluted white vinegar or powdered laundry soap, mixed with just enough water to create a paste.

If you want to avoid having to use chlorine bleach or chemical fungicides, the best way to deal with mildew is to prevent it in the first place. Always keep the bathroom well-ventilated during and after showering. Run the exhaust fan, open the door a little, or crack a window.

Never leave a wet shower curtain open; mildew will grow in the damp folds. If you see the beginnings of mildew on the curtain, launder it immediately in the hottest water the fabric can take; then allow to dry in full sunlight.

Bathtubs, enameled and porcelain A powdered cleanser with oxygen bleach, made of nonabrasive finely ground silica (sand), is a great alternative to harsh chemical cleaners. When oxygen bleach comes in contact with air and water, it literally oxidizes dirt and grime.

Bathtubs, fiberglass Never use abrasive cleaners or scrubbers on fiberglass—even gentle rubbing with abrasives will scratch the surface. Instead, try vinegar or a mixture of baking soda and mild dish soap. (Rinse well between remedies, if you decide to try one after the other.)

TIP | EDITING YOUR MEDICINE CHEST

As long as you'll need to empty your medicine cabinet, under sink cabinets, and drawers to wipe them out, take an extra minute to sort through things before you put them back. Spring cleaning season is a great time to get rid of old prescriptions, unwanted toiletries, and expired sunscreens, which lose their effectiveness after one year. Be sure to keep all medications, even expired ones, away from children and pets. And make a list of things you need to replace, like adhesive bandages and pain relievers, so you'll have them when needed.

Drains Soap, hair, and shaving creams are the usual suspects in most bathtub and sink clogs. It's much easier to remedy a slow drain than one that's completely stopped. At the first signs of sluggishness, pour a kettle full of boiling water down the drain. If that isn't enough to clear the drain, try half a cup of hydrogen peroxide from your medicine cabinet. Wait ten to fifteen minutes, then follow it with boiling water. If you don't have peroxide handy, use a half cup of baking soda, followed by one cup of white vinegar. Wait up to thirty minutes and follow with boiling water.

Showerhead residue If hard water has left a ghostly film on your showerhead, unscrew it, and soak it overnight in a bowl of white vinegar. Then simply rinse and reinstall.

Shower curtains Launder your shower curtain with detergent in the warmest water the material will tolerate. Plastic and vinyl curtains will be very wet after the wash cycle. Remove immediately, to prevent wrinkles, and wrap in a large towel to transfer back to the bathroom. Hang to drip dry.

Toilets Raise the lid and seat and pour a bucket of water briskly into the bowl. This will lower the water level. Apply toilet cleaner or laundry borax and scrub with a brush. Flush immediately or leave overnight to remove tough stains.

CELEBRATE A JOB WELL DONE :: *A pleasant fragrance is especially important in the bathroom—so a delightfully scented soap or candle is an essential luxury.*

3. THE LAUNDRY ROOM

Unless your laundry area is located in a public part of your home, you probably don't think about cleaning it throughout the year. But spring cleaning your laundry room gives you a chance to excavate missing socks and rid your home of lint bunnies—the bigger, more ferocious cousins of the common household dust bunny.

Cleaning your laundry room is a simple job, so you probably won't need to budget a lot of time. Start with a notebook and make a list of what needs to be done or use the following master list as a guide.

MASTER LIST | LAUNDRY ROOM

Remove cobwebs in corners

Dust and wipe washer, dryer, and other surfaces

Collect wire hangers to return to dry cleaner for recycling

Launder laundry bags

Check dowels on wooden drying rack to see if any rough spots need sanding

Sanitize washing machine

Clean out utility tub

Clean out dryer duct

Sweep up dust and lint (especially behind washer and dryer)

Mop floor

After you determine what needs to be done in your laundry room, identify the tools and time you'll need for each task.

SAMPLE PLAN | LAUNDRY ROOM = 1 HOUR, 22 MINUTES

TASK	TOOLS ($ = need to buy)	TIME
Remove cobwebs	Vacuum cleaner with hose extension	10 min
Wipe down surfaces	Spray cleaner, sponge	10 min
Sanitize washing machine	Oxygen bleach	2 min
Clean dryer duct	Vacuum cleaner with hose extension	30 min
Sweep and mop floor	Broom, dustpan, mop, bucket, all-purpose cleaner	30 min

Dryer duct Even though you empty out the lint trap after every dryer load, some lint will make its way through to the dryer duct. Accumulated lint deposits will hamper the performance and energy efficiency of your dryer and may even be a fire hazard. To check your duct, simply inspect the vent on the exterior of your house. If a lot of lint has accumulated around the vent, it's probably a good idea to clean the duct. Go back inside and detach the duct from the dryer. (Check your owner's manual if this looks tricky.) Then clear the duct with the hose attachment on your vacuum cleaner. If there's only a little lint in the duct and around the exterior vent, yearly cleaning is probably unnecessary.

Sock strategies Socks disappear. This appears to be some kind of inevitable cosmic law. It doesn't matter if you live alone in total order and serenity, with a houseful of roommates, or amid the chaos of family life. You will lose socks—and you will always lose them one at a time.

There are steps you can take to keep orphaned socks to a minimum. Many housewares merchants sell plastic clips that keep pairs together as they travel through the washer and dryer. Some people just use ordinary safety pins to pin the cuffs together. If you ever notice someone sporting a pin on one sock cuff, it's a safe bet that he or she takes sock sorting very seriously.

For households where pinning and clipping aren't practical, the sock basket is an easy solution. Every sock that gets separated from its mate gets tossed into a basket near the dryer. Once a year, the basket is emptied, and all unmated socks are discarded.

Washing machine To sanitize your washer tub, set the machine for a full-size, hot-water wash cycle. Add a cup of oxygen bleach. (Do not add laundry to this cycle.) Allow the water to drain, then run a rinse cycle of clear water.

CELEBRATE A JOB WELL DONE :: *Scented clothespins add a touch of fragrance to line-dried clothes and linens. Or slip fragrant drawer liner papers into stacks of sheets and towels.*

4. THE BASEMENT

If rainy days are keeping you indoors, give your basement a once-over for spring. It's a job worth doing, even if no one ever sees it but you. Musty basement smells can affect the air quality throughout your home, especially in hot, muggy weather.

Grab your notebook, turn on all the lights, and take a ceiling-to-floor inventory of what needs to be done. Brace yourself. This could get ugly. Maintain your composure and use the master list below to get you started.

MASTER LIST | BASEMENT

Remove cobwebs in corners

Change burned out bulbs

Identify unneeded household
goods for charity donations

Wash walls

Empty dehumidifier bucket
and change filter

Replace furnace filter

Inspect air conditioner

Sweep floor

Mop floor

Once you decide what your basement needs, determine the tools and time you'll need to accomplish each task.

SAMPLE PLAN | BASEMENT = 3 HOURS, 5 MINUTES

TASK	TOOLS ($ = need to buy)	TIME
Remove cobwebs	Broom	20 min
Wash walls	All-purpose cleaner, bucket, sponge mop	60 min
Collect giveaway goods	Big trash bags	60 min
Sweep floor	Broom	15 min
Mop floor	Mop, bucket, all-purpose cleaner	30 min

Open the windows, if possible, for fresh air. Plug in a portable stereo (see page 12 for music suggestions). Take a deep breath. And begin.

CELEBRATE A JOB WELL DONE :: *Invest in some inexpensive shelving to organize the items you store in your basement. Getting boxes up off the floor makes seldom-used belongings easier to find and protects them from dampness. Line shelves with drawer liner paper to freshen the air.*

YOUR BASEMENT AND THE BARCELONA TEST

For many of us, the basement serves as a holding area for unfinished projects, broken appliances, and things we forgot to return to the store. Over time, they gather dust, absorb dampness, and acquire that funny brownish-gray basement smell. This can go on for years, without incident. But eventually all this stuff will get in your way. Maybe you'll need to have your hot water heater serviced—and spend half a morning digging for it first. Maybe someone will offer you the job of your dreams in Barcelona, so you'll have to put your house on the market and offer guided tours of your basement to prospective buyers.

A tidy, well-edited basement can make it far easier to cope with some of life's not-so-little surprises. So, as long as you're spring cleaning anyway, use the occasion to get rid of things you no longer need. Simply consider each forlorn, forgotten item in turn and ask yourself the following question: "Would I be willing to pay someone to pack this up and move it to Barcelona?"

If it's a black-and-white television, probably not. If it's your grandmother's antique wing chair, maybe. If it's a box of holiday ornaments, probably yes.

Even if the chances of your moving to Barcelona are pretty slim, the Barcelona Test is well worth the hour or so it will take. The less cluttered the basement, the easier it will be to clean. And you don't have to throw away everything that fails the test. Plenty of charities welcome old appliances and other things in need of a little tender loving care.

The items you decide to keep also will need a little care. To prevent fire and water damage, be sure to keep everything well away from your furnace, hot water heater, washer, and dryer. Make sure there's always an unobstructed pathway to each appliance.

Once your basement is clean, consider giving it a fresh coat of paint. If dampness is a problem, think about installing a dehumidifier to prevent molds and mildew from undoing all your hard work.

AFTERWORD

SOME PERFECTLY GOOD REASONS TO NEGLECT SPRING CLEANING

Just because we make cleaning products doesn't mean our homes are perfect. We've used just about all these excuses at one time or another. The only excuse we don't endorse is: "No one will notice the difference but me." A serenely clean home is one of the nicest ways you can care for yourself. The fact that you'll notice and enjoy it is the whole point of spring cleaning.

Nevertheless, if you need an excuse, feel free to try one of ours:

:: The house will only be dirty again tomorrow. And that will just about break my heart.

:: I'm waiting for my children to grow up and leave home.

:: I'm waiting for my spouse to grow up and leave home.

:: If I have to choose between cleaning and sleeping, I will always choose sleeping.

:: I just had a baby. (This excuse actually has a fairly long shelf life, but it definitely expires when your child is tall enough to push a broom.)

:: I keep my house messy on purpose to make my mother crazy.

:: I think I'm coming down with something. In fact, I'm sure of it.

:: If I put everything away, I won't know where to find it.

:: I just did it last year.

:: It doesn't look so bad. (My husband says this every year.)